YOUNG DISCOVERERS

SOLIDS AND LIQUIDS

DAVID GLOVER

Kingfisher Books

NEW YORK

KINGFISHER
Larousse Kingfisher Chambers Inc.
95 Madison Avenue
New York, New York 10016

First American edition 1993
10 9 8 7 6 5 4 3 2 (HC)
10 9 8 7 6 5 4   (PB)
10 9 8 7 6 5 4 3 2 1 (LIB. BDG.)
© Grisewood & Dempsey Ltd. 1993

Library of Congress
Cataloging-in-Publication Data

Glover, David
    Solids and liquids / David Glover. —
1st American ed.
        p.   cm. — (Young discoverers)
    Includes index.
    Summary: Examines the composition and
strength of materials, both solid and liquid,
and features experiments, including
chemical reactions.
    1. Matter—Juvenile literature. 2. Matter
—Experiments—Juvenile literature.
[1. Matter.   2. Matter—Experiments.
3. Experiments.] I. Title.   II. Series.
QC173.16.G56 1993
530.4—dc20   92-40214 CIP AC

ISBN 1-85697-845-1 (HC)
ISBN 1-85697-934-2 (PB)
ISBN 1-85697-634-3 (LIB. BDG.)

Series editor: Sue Nicholson
Designer: Ben White
Picture research: Elaine Willis
Cover design: Dave West
Cover illustration: Kuo Kang Chen
Illustrators: Kuo Kang Chen pp.2, 8-9, 10-11,
    16-17, 24, 25 (left); David Evans, Kathy
    Jakeman Illustration p.22 (top); Chris Forsey
    pp. 4-5; Hayward Art Group pp.6 (bot.), 25,
    27; Kevin Maddison pp.6 (top), 7 (top), 12, 15,
    18-19 (centre), 23, 29, 30-31; Janos Marffy,
    Kathy Jakeman Illustration pp.7 (bot.), 13, 14,
    18 (bot. left), 19, 20-21, 22 (bot.), 26, 28
Photographs: David Glover pp.13, 18; J.Allan
    Cash Ltd p.24; Robert Harding Picture Library
    p.27; Hutchison Library p.31; ZEFA pp.10, 14,
    20, 26, 29

Printed in Hong Kong

About This Book

This book tells you about materials — the solids, liquids, and gases from which everything around us is made. It also has lots of experiments and things to look out for.

You should be able to find nearly everything you need for the experiments around your home. You may have to buy some items, but they are all cheap and easy to find. Sometimes you will need to ask an adult to help you, such as when heating up hot liquids or drilling holes.

Be a Smart Scientist
● Before you begin an experiment, read the instructions carefully and collect all the things you need.
● Put on some old clothes or wear a smock.
● When you have finished, clear everything away, especially sharp things such as knives and scissors, and wash your hands.

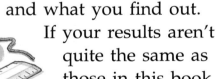

● Keep a record of what you do and what you find out. If your results aren't quite the same as those in this book don't worry. See if you can work out what has happened, and why.

Contents

What's It Made Of?

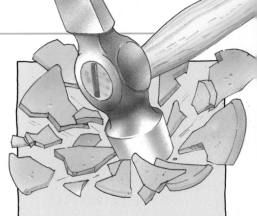

Have you ever wondered what makes one thing different from another? A ball, a drop of water, the wind, are all very different because they are made from different materials.

Most materials are solid, such as metal and wood. Solids don't change shape unless you cut, bend, or break them. Some solids, like glass, break easily. Some, like stone and many plastics, are very strong.

Other materials are liquid. Water is a liquid. It flows and doesn't have a shape of its own.

Solids don't last forever. Glass breaks easily. Cloth and paper rot. Stone wears away; and some metals rust (see page 27).

 **Eye-Spy**

Make a collection of different solids and decide whether they are made of wood, metal, plastic, stone, rubber, glass, or something else.

Here are five solid materials that look and feel different.
1. Metals are strong. They can be sharpened into blades for cutting.

4

A third kind of material is gas. Air is a gas. You can't see it and it is so thin you can pass your hand through it. Yet you can feel air when it blows over your face and hands.

2. Rubber is light and grips well. It is also springy and returns to its original shape when it is stretched.

3. Glass is transparent (you can see through it), but it breaks if you drop it.

4. Most clothes are woven from fibers (fine threads). Woven fibers are strong and flexible — they bend easily.

5. Plastic is strong, light, and waterproof. It doesn't rot or rust and it can be made into any shape.

Do it yourself

Look more closely at your collection of solids through a magnifying glass.

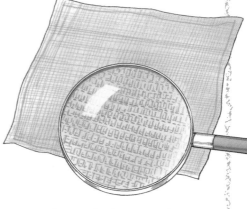

See how cloth is made up of tiny woven threads. Glass, metal, and many plastics look shiny and smooth. Some rocks are made up of differently colored shiny grains.

metal

rock

glass

plastic

wood

5

Materials All Around

Everything we use is made from materials. Some, like cotton, come from plants. Others, like wool, come from animals. Many buildings are made from stone which is cut or dug from the ground. Cotton, wool, and stone are all natural materials.

Some natural materials can be made into other things. Oil can be made into plastics. Coal can be made into paint or soap. Coal and oil are called raw materials. Plastic is a manufactured, or artificial, material.

All plants and animals are made from many different materials. Two of the main ones are water and carbon. (Carbon is the black stuff in the middle of pencils.) In every human body there is enough water to fill 4 buckets and enough carbon to make over 1,000 pencils.

Oil is formed from the remains of ancient plants and animals. We drill for oil and dig for coal under the Earth's surface, through layers of rock.

Wood into Coal

1. Millions of years ago the Earth was covered by thick forests and swamps.
2. Fallen trees were gradually buried by thick layers of mud and sand.
3. The squashed wood slowly turned into coal.

① ② ③
coal

oil rig

coal mine

One of the main gases that makes up air is oxygen. All living things need oxygen. We must breathe oxygen gas to stay alive. Plants "breathe out" lifegiving oxygen.

When materials like coal and oil burn they use oxygen from the air and give out heat (see next page).

What's in Air?

Air is mostly made up of the two gases nitrogen and oxygen. It also contains water in the form of a gas (water vapor) and tiny bits of salt, dust, and dirt.

Do it yourself

See how materials use oxygen when they burn. You'll need a small candle, a saucer, some water, and a glass jar.

1. Ask an adult to stick the candle to the bottom of the saucer with some melted candle wax, and then light the candle for you.

2. Pour about half an inch (1 cm) of water into the bottom of the saucer. Turn a glass jar upside down and carefully lower it over the candle. The glass should just sit in the water. Watch what happens to the candle flame.

saucer or jar lid

glass

water level

watch the candle flame

How It Works

The candle needs oxygen gas to burn. It therefore goes out when it has used up most of the oxygen in the glass. The water rises in the glass to take the space of the used oxygen.

7

Melting and Mixing

Have you ever sat in front of a roaring log fire? The wood on the fire uses oxygen as it burns. The burning wood gives off heat and turns into ash.

Heat changes materials. It can change solids into liquids and liquids into gases. Heat can make things melt, make them cook, and set them on fire.

Eye-Spy

See how chocolate melts and goes runny on a hot day — it changes from a solid to a liquid.

Do it yourself

Find out how heat affects different materials. You will need three saucers, some ice, a chocolate bar, some butter, and a wax candle.

Arrange a piece of each material around the edges of the saucers (You'll need three pieces of each material.) Put one saucer in the refrigerator, one in a cool room, and one in sunlight or next to a hot fire.

- Which materials melt?

- Which go soft?

- Which stay solid?

	chocolate	ice	butter	wax
melts				
gets soft				
stays solid				

✔✔ hot spot
✔ cool room
● refrigerator

You could use a chart like this to record your results. Try testing some other materials in the same way.

Do it yourself

See how some liquids will mix together while others don't mix at all, and how some solids dissolve (mix into a liquid).

eye dropper

food coloring

shake mixture hard

sugar

sand

instant coffee

flour

detergent

salt

Mixing

Stir some milk into hot coffee to see how the milk and coffee mix to a brown color. Now try dropping a blob of ink or food coloring into some water to see how they mix together.

Unmixing

Pour equal amounts of cooking oil and water into a clear plastic jar with a screw-on top. Screw on the top and shake the jar hard to try and mix the contents together. Leave the bottle to stand and watch how the oil floats on top of the water in a layer.

Dissolving

When you stir sugar into a hot drink it dissolves. Most things dissolve more easily in warm water than in cold. Try stirring the things on the right into hot and then cold water and see what happens.

Mixing Things Together

All solids, liquids, and gases are made up of chemicals. When some chemicals are mixed together they react, or change, and new chemicals are made.

Did you know that cooking is a kind of chemical reaction? When you bake a cake in the oven all the things you put into the mixture react together to make a solid. Beating the cake mixture is important because it mixes in air — it's the air bubbles that make the cake light and fluffy.

Chemistry

Chemistry is the name for the part of science that is all about what things are made of and how they can be changed.

👁 Eye-Spy

Ask an adult to boil some red cabbage and then help you to pour off some of the cabbage water into two dishes. Add lemon juice to one dish and baking powder to the second. See how the chemical reactions make the water change color.

red cabbage water on its own

with baking powder

with lemon juice

Do it yourself

Make a chemical reaction that will power a rocket. You'll need a small plastic bottle with a screw-on top, a long piece of smooth string, a plastic straw, tape, tissue paper, vinegar, and baking powder.

1. Thread the string through the straw and stretch it out as shown. Pour an inch of vinegar into the bottle and tape the bottle to the straw.

2. Put a few teaspoonfuls of baking powder into some tissue paper and wrap it into a parcel.

3. Gently slide the parcel into the bottle, trying to keep it out of the vinegar until you have screwed on the top of the bottle.

4. Give the bottle a shake and wait for takeoff!

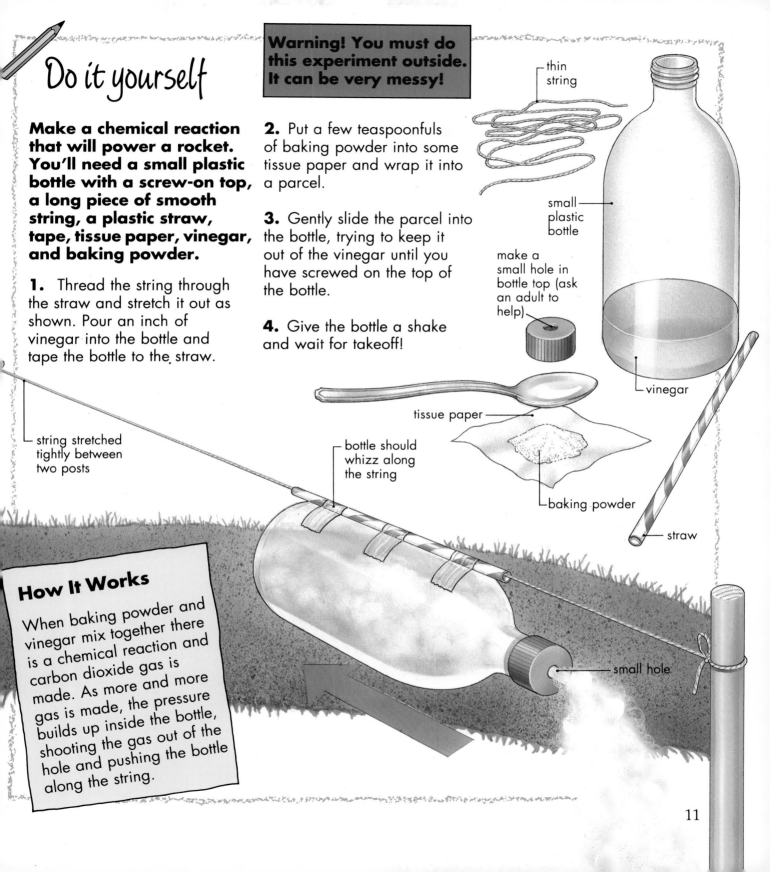

thin string

small plastic bottle

make a small hole in bottle top (ask an adult to help)

vinegar

tissue paper

baking powder

straw

string stretched tightly between two posts

bottle should whizz along the string

small hole

How It Works

When baking powder and vinegar mix together there is a chemical reaction and carbon dioxide gas is made. As more and more gas is made, the pressure builds up inside the bottle, shooting the gas out of the hole and pushing the bottle along the string.

11

Stone, Wood, and Clay

Thousands of years ago, people used the natural materials around them to make the things they needed. For example, sticks and stones were used to make tools and weapons. As time passed, people started to make other things. Logs were hollowed out to make canoes. Reeds were woven into baskets, and clay was made into pots.

Stone and Wood

Stone and wood have different properties — they look, feel, and behave in different ways. Stone is heavy and will sink in water. It is difficult to cut and it doesn't burn or rot.

Wood is light and will float in water. It is easily cut but it burns and can rot.

Because stone and wood have different properties, they can be used in different ways. Buildings made from stone last for hundreds of years. Wood is good for making boats. It can also be burned as a fuel.

Do it yourself

Try making thumb and coil pots from clay. You could use them to keep things in.

Thumb Pots

Roll a piece of clay into a ball about the size of your fist. Stick your thumb into the middle of the ball to make a hole. Then turn the clay around your thumb while you shape the outside with your fingers.

Coil Pots

Roll out some long, thin clay snakes. Cut out a circle to make a base. Then coil the snakes around and around to make the sides.

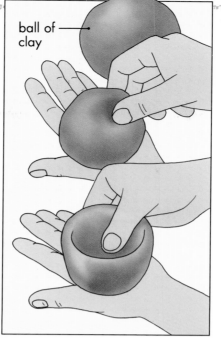

ball of clay

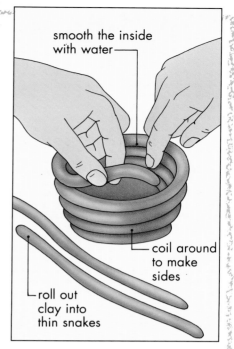

smooth the inside with water

coil around to make sides

roll out clay into thin snakes

If you can, bake your pots in a very hot oven called a kiln. Perhaps your school has one.

Firing a Pot

Before it is baked or "fired," a clay pot is very weak and crumbly — like a cracker. Heat hardens the clay, making it much stronger and waterproof.

Left: Ever since early times, potters have used a wheel to make pots. As the wheel turns, the potter shapes the clay with his hands.

13

Making Tools

Long ago, people chipped flints from huge stones and used them to make arrows, spearheads, and sharp blades for knives and axes. Their tools did similar jobs to tools we use today, but they were more clumsy and harder to handle.

Metal Tools

Most modern tools have sharp, light metal blades. Some have motors to make them work faster.

Do it yourself

Try making your own tools with sticks, stones, and strong string.

You could use pebbles to make hammerheads. Sticks can be cut into tool handles or digging sticks. But be careful — ask an adult to help you cut them.

If you live in a chalky area, you may be able to find pieces of flint. Flint is a glassy, hard stone found in some rocks. You could then try making a flint ax or scraper like the ones shown here.

Try doing different jobs with your tools. Are they easy to use?

scraper

flint ax

put stone in fork of a branch and bind the wood around it with string

hammer

digging stick

stick

stones

strong string

14

Later, people began to make better tools from metals. They discovered a way of heating certain types of rocks so they could get copper out of them. Then they found that when they mixed tin with the hot copper it made a new material — bronze.

Copper and tin are quite soft and flexible on their own, but bronze is hard enough to be used for sharp knife blades and ax heads.

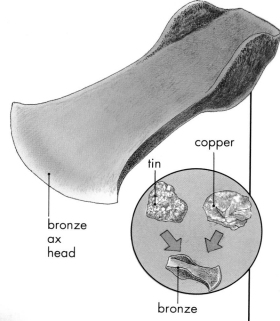

bronze ax head

tin

copper

bronze

The Bronze Age

The Bronze Age started about 5,000 years ago. Bronze tools and ornaments have been found in the Middle East, China, and Europe.

The Iron Age

About 3,000 years ago people found a way of separating iron from rocks. Iron is stronger than bronze. Iron tools last longer and can be sharpened more easily.

👁 Eye-Spy

Visit a museum and look out for stone, bronze, and iron tools and weapons. You'll find that the wooden handles have rotted away.

15

Metal Magic

We now use more than fifty kinds of metal and most of them are found in rocks. Some of the more common ones are iron, copper, tin, aluminum, silver, gold, and chromium. As each type of metal has different properties it can be used in different ways. Some metals are better for making cars and others for making coins.

Strong Metal

Steel is very strong. Steel wires and girders are often used to make bridges. Steel is mainly iron with a small amount of carbon mixed in it to make the iron stronger and harder.

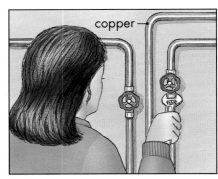

Flexible Metal

Pure metals (metals that have not been mixed with anything else) are quite soft and bendy. They are used for wires or pipes.

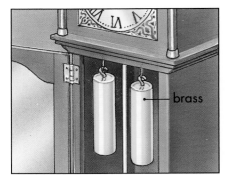

Heavy Metal

Nearly all metals are heavier than water, so they sink. Lead and brass are two of the heaviest metals. They are often used to make weights.

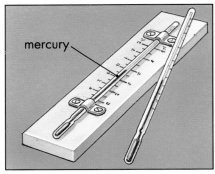

Liquid Metal

All metals melt into thick liquids when they get very hot. Mercury is special. It is the only metal that stays liquid when it is cool.

Do it yourself

Use these four tests to help you decide whether something is made from metal.

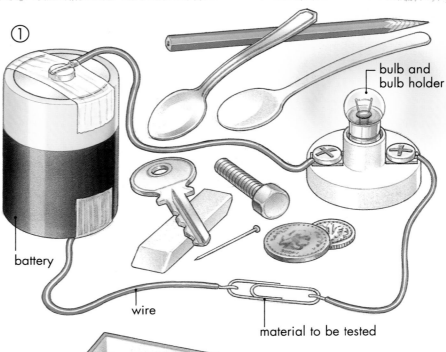

① battery

bulb and bulb holder

wire

material to be tested

1. Does it carry electricity?
Test your material with a battery, a bulb, and two wires. All metal conducts, or carries, electricity. For the test to work, the wires must touch bare metal, not paint.

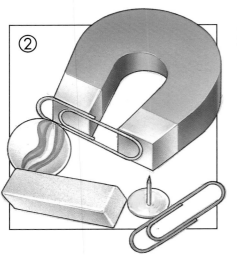

②

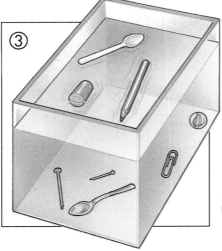

③

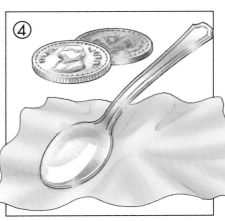

④

2. Is it magnetic?
If your material is attracted or "pulled" by a magnet, then it contains the metal iron. If not, then it may still be a metal like copper or aluminum (which aren't magnetic).

3. Does it float or sink?
All common metals are heavier than water, so they will sink. Therefore, if your material floats on water it is not a metal and must be made from something else.

4. Can it be polished?
Most metals can be polished to a bright shine. Metals shine in light so they can be used as mirrors. If you can see through your material, then it isn't a metal.

Useful Plastics

Plastics are not natural materials. They're made in factories from the chemicals found in oil. The chemicals are heated in steel tanks which are rather like huge pressure cookers. When the chemicals stick together, new plastic materials are made.

Plastics are lighter and more flexible than metals, but they aren't as strong. Plastics can melt or burn when they are heated. An important property of plastic is that it doesn't conduct electricity, so plastic is wrapped around electric wire to make the wire safer.

Plastic gets soft when it's heated, so it can be made into all sorts of shapes, like these toys.

👁 Eye-Spy

Put a yogurt container in a bowl. Then ask an adult to pour some very hot water over it. Watch how the plastic container softens and changes shape.

boiling water

yogurt container

Plastic canoes and safety helmets don't crack or shatter when they get knocked.

Do it yourself

Make some rubbery plastic at home from milk and vinegar.

1. Ask an adult to warm some creamy milk in a pan. When the milk is simmering, slowly stir in a few teaspoonfuls of vinegar.

creamy milk

vinegar

wash in cold water

2. Keep stirring, but just before the mixture becomes rubbery add some food coloring.

3. Let the plastic cool and wash it under cold running water.

Stretchy, Strong, or Brittle?

Find some different kinds of plastic and try bending and stretching them. Are they stretchy and weak or stretchy and strong? Or are they brittle (do they snap easily)?

plastic spoon

homemade plastic

plastic can holders

plastic wrap

Springy Rubber

Rubber is made from a white juice, called latex, which comes from rubber trees. At factories, the liquid latex is made into solid rubber by adding an acid — just as you added vinegar (an acid) to the milk in the activity on page 19. Then the rubber is squeezed, dried, and shaped.

Rubber is a useful material because it is so elastic. It can be stretched and squashed and it will still bounce back into shape.

Collecting Latex

Latex drips slowly into a collecting cup from grooves cut into the bark of a rubber tree. About one cupful of latex is collected each time.

👁 Eye-Spy

See how different types of material slide less easily (make more friction) than others.

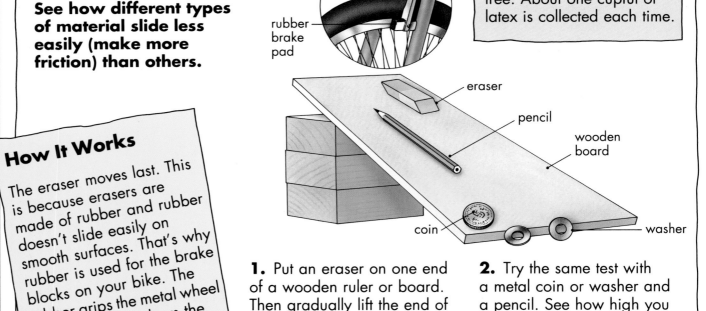

rubber brake pad

eraser

pencil

wooden board

coin

washer

How It Works

The eraser moves last. This is because erasers are made of rubber and rubber doesn't slide easily on smooth surfaces. That's why rubber is used for the brake blocks on your bike. The rubber grips the metal wheel rim and friction slows the wheel down.

1. Put an eraser on one end of a wooden ruler or board. Then gradually lift the end of the wood until the eraser just starts to slip.

2. Try the same test with a metal coin or washer and a pencil. See how high you have to lift the wood before each material starts to slip.

Do it yourself

Make your own rubber-powered machines.

Spool Tank

Thread a rubber band through the middle of an empty spool. Secure the band at both ends, as shown in drawings 1 and 2.

Wind up the band by turning the longer piece of wood until you cannot turn it any more. Place it on a smooth surface, then let go!

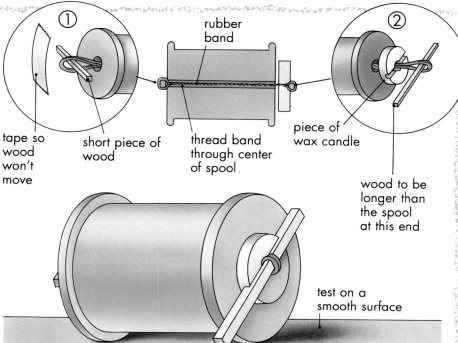

① tape so wood won't move

short piece of wood

rubber band

thread band through center of spool

② piece of wax candle

wood to be longer than the spool at this end

test on a smooth surface

Rubber Roadster

This roadster is also powered by a twisted rubber band. Here, though, the band turns a propeller — like the ones found in modeling kits. The propeller is attached to the rubber band with a hook that runs through the balsa wood and two metal washers. (You should be able to find the washers around your home, or you can buy them quite cheaply from a hardware store.)

Why not hold a competition to design the fastest rubber-powered vehicle!

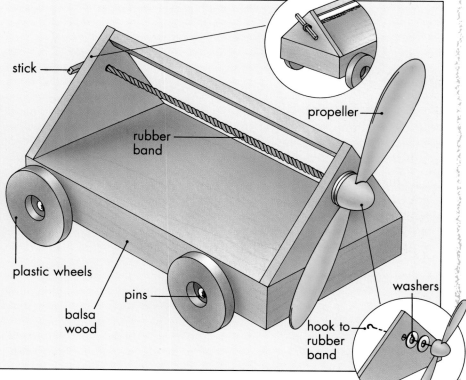

stick

rubber band

propeller

plastic wheels

pins

balsa wood

hook to rubber band

washers

Flexible Fibers

Fibers are simply long, thin, flexible strands or threads. We use both natural fibers, from plants and animals, and artificial fibers, from oil and coal. Cotton comes from the seed pods of the cotton plant and wool comes from sheep. String can be made from plant fibers, and nylon is made from the chemicals in oil.

Plant, animal, and artificial fibers can all be woven to make different kinds of cloth. Look at the labels in your clothes. Some will be made from mixtures of fibers, like cotton and nylon, or cotton and polyester.

A hair is a fiber. Animal fur is just a thick coat of hair. It traps tiny pockets of air between the fibers, keeping in the warmth.

👁 Eye-Spy

Collect some different fibers and look at them through a magnifying glass. Are they smooth or rough, thick or thin? Wool and string are much rougher than nylon.

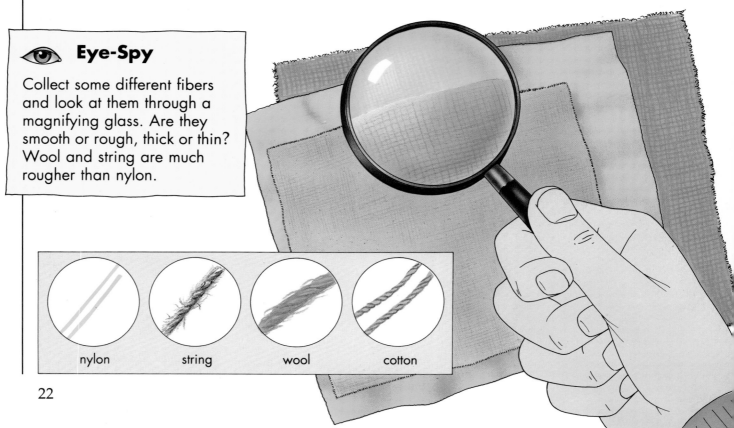

nylon   string   wool   cotton

Paper is made from fibers, too. Usually it's made from wood fibers. The wood is separated into fibers by crushing it to a pulp in water. The pulp is then squeezed into thin sheets and dried.

If you look at a piece of cloth and a piece of tissue paper under a magnifying glass you can see the fibers clearly. The fibers in cloth are woven together evenly. But the fibers in paper are just squashed together in a jumble.

secure with rubber band

yogurt container

Making It Waterproof

Cloth is not usually waterproof because of all the tiny holes between the fibers. Try making a piece of cloth waterproof by rubbing it with candle wax to block the holes. See if it has worked by wrapping the cloth around the top of a container filled with water then tipping the container upside down.

Do it yourself

Try weaving a piece of cloth with some yarn.

1. Cut a row of triangular grooves in opposite sides of a piece of thick cardboard.

2. Wind the yarn around the cardboard as shown. This is called the warp.

3. Thread the needle with another strand of wool and weave it in and out of the warp thread. This is the weft.

4. When you've finished, knot the end and cut the threads so that you can remove the cardboard.

stiff cardboard

warp

weft

23

Strong But Brittle

Glass is made from sand — just like the sand on a beach. The sand is heated with limestone and other materials until they melt and mix together. The red-hot mixture is poured into different shapes. It then cools and sets to solid glass.

Glass is a very useful material. As it's transparent, we use it for windows and glasses. It's also waterproof and easy to clean, so it is used to make bottles and jars.

Breaking Glass

Although glass is strong and hard, it is also brittle. This means that it can shatter easily. A glass bottle can carry a heavy weight without breaking, but a sudden knock can make it shatter. Have you ever dropped a glass and seen it break into sharp pieces? (Don't test this out though, you could hurt yourself!)

When broken glass is especially dangerous, a special safety glass is used (see next page).

Left: Some glass bowls or ornaments are made by glass blowers. They pick up a blob of soft glass on the end of a hollow tube. Then they blow into the tube and the glass blows up like a balloon.

Making It Strong

A tennis racket must be strong enough to hit a ball without breaking. A bridge needs be able to take the weight of all the traffic that uses it. Things must be made so that they are safe and strong enough to last. To make something strong, you must use a strong material and you must make it into a strong shape.

Wonderful Webs

The silken strands in a spider's web are just 0.0001 inch thick but they are stronger than steel of the same thickness!

Concrete Strength

Many buildings are made out of concrete, which is a mixture of cement, water, and gravel or sand. As concrete can crack if it is stretched, it is often reinforced (made stronger) by thin steel rods that are set into the mixture.

Safety Glass

Car windshields are usually made of safety glass. The glass may still shatter but the pieces won't fly into the driver's face because they're held in place by a sheet of clear plastic sandwiched between two glass sheets.

Carbon Fibers

Fibers made from carbon are flexible, light, and strong. They are used to make parts of bikes, tennis rackets, and aircraft bodies. Carbon fibers weigh about a quarter as much as steel, but they are twice as strong.

Do it yourself

See if you can design a strong bridge shape.

1. First try experimenting with paper bridge shapes. Paper is much too flexible to make a flat bridge, but if you fold the paper the bridge can be made much stiffer and stronger. Three strong bridge shapes are shown below.

Above: Sydney Harbour Bridge in Australia is made from steel. It carries eight lanes of traffic and two railroad tracks.

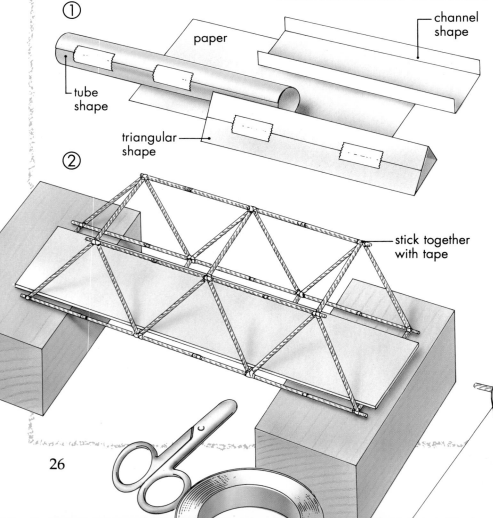

① paper

tube shape

channel shape

triangular shape

②

stick together with tape

2. Try making a bridge frame out of plastic straws. Join the straws by pushing the end of one into the end of another, then taping them together. You can test your bridge's strength by seeing whether it can take the weight of a yogurt container filled with sand.

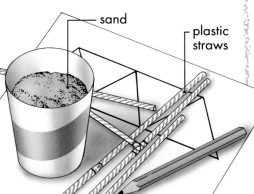

sand

plastic straws

Rusting and Rotting

Nearly all materials wear out. Most do not last forever. Have you ever left a bike in the rain? Did it go rusty? Iron rusts when it gets damp — it reacts with water and oxygen in the air and eventually bits of the metal crumble to a brown powder.

Wood rots if it gets too damp. Fungus grows on it and the wood loses its strength. Even stone can wear away. It can crack and crumble in frost and rain.

Some types of rock are softer than others. Here, the continuous pounding of waves has gradually worn away the cliffs.

👁 Eye-Spy

Look out for insect holes in old furniture and trees.
Some insects eat wood — woodworms and termites can destroy whole buildings. There is even a bee that makes holes in brick walls. The masonry bee burrows into the mortar between bricks to lay its eggs.

Gold is the only metal that doesn't rust even when it is buried in the ground for thousands of years. Because it stays so bright, gold is called the "noble metal."

Do it yourself

Find out what makes iron rust. You'll need four iron nails, four glass jars (one with a lid), and some nail polish.

① tap water

② boiled water

screw-on top

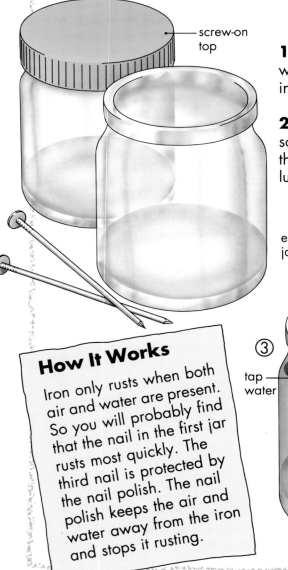

1. Fill one jar to the brim with water and drop a nail into it.

2. Ask an adult to boil some water for you. Leave the water to cool until it is lukewarm. Pour the water into another jar, making sure that it is full to the brim. Drop the second nail into the jar and screw on the lid. (Ordinary water has air in it. Boiling the water gets rid of the air and putting a lid on the jar prevents fresh air from getting into the jar.)

3. Paint the third nail all over with nail polish. Drop this nail into a jar of ordinary water. Don't put a lid on the jar.

4. Drop the fourth nail into an empty jar. Again, don't screw on a lid.

Look at the jars every day to see which nails are getting rusty and which aren't.

④ empty jar

③ tap water

painted nail

nail polish

How It Works

Iron only rusts when both air and water are present. So you will probably find that the nail in the first jar rusts most quickly. The third nail is protected by the nail polish. The nail polish keeps the air and water away from the iron and stops it rusting.

28

Using It Again

Have you ever counted how many glass bottles, metal cans, or plastic containers are thrown away in your house in a week, or a month? It all adds up to a lot of garbage.

Instead of throwing away glass, metal, and plastic, you can help the environment by using them again. Recyling reduces the amount of garbage we make and saves energy and money.

New From Old

This recycling plant in Germany sorts out different metals. The steel will be reused to make new containers.

Do it yourself

See which things rot away.

Dig a hole and bury a soda can, a glass jar, a plastic container, paper, and some apple slices. Mark the place with a stick. Dig it up after two weeks.

Don't forget to take your garbage away after two weeks is up!

How It Works

Worms and other tiny creatures will have begun to eat the food and paper. These things are biodegradable. The glass, plastic, and metal would just lie in the soil for years.

Do it yourself

Recycle the things you use. Every little bit helps so if you don't already recycle your garbage — start now!

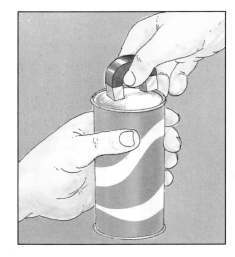

● Test your empty soda cans with a magnet to see whether they are steel or aluminum. Steel will be attracted by the magnet, aluminum will not.

● Wash steel cans and glass bottles and jars and take them to a collection point.

● Use clean, empty plastic containers for storing food or for growing plants and seedlings. Wash and reuse plastic bags wherever possible.

Save a Tree!

Every year everyone throws away more than 300 pounds of paper. That's two trees worth of newspapers, tissues, and all the other paper things in the garbage can.

All around the world forests are shrinking. The rain forests are in most danger. Not enough new trees are planted to replace the ones that are being cut down.

- Open envelopes carefully so you can reuse them to send your letters. Buy gummed labels to stick over the old address.

- Buy recycled paper for painting and drawing.

- Save and pack up old papers and comics so that the paper can be recycled.

Planting Trees

In this project in Ecuador, South America, fast-growing eucalyptus trees will be planted to replace trees that have been cut down and burned.

recycled paper

labels

Index